A Pictorial Celebration
THE AMERICAN WOMAN

By The Winners Of The Parade-Kodak National Photo Contest
Introduction By Walter Anderson
Continuum • New York

1989

The Continuum Publishing Company
370 Lexington Avenue
New York, NY 10017

Copyright © 1989 by Parade Publications, Inc.

Design by Ira Yoffe

Printed in the United States of America

Library of Congress Cataloging-in-Publication Data
The American woman: a pictorial celebration by the winners
of the Parade—Kodak National Photo Contest
introduction by Walter Anderson.
p.   cm.
ISBN 0-8264-0447-2
1. Photography of women.
I. Anderson, Walter.
TR681. W6A46 1989
779' .24' 0973—dc 20   89-31699 CIP

►
Cristina M. Barr on the job as power-plant mechanic in Trenton, N.J. Photo by her mother, Christina E. Jordan.

►►
On following page: Matching set: Hope Houston, 6, and sister Nancy, 8, of Bellaire, Tex.—pincurled and arm-in-arm. Photo by their father, Jerry Houston.

Introduction

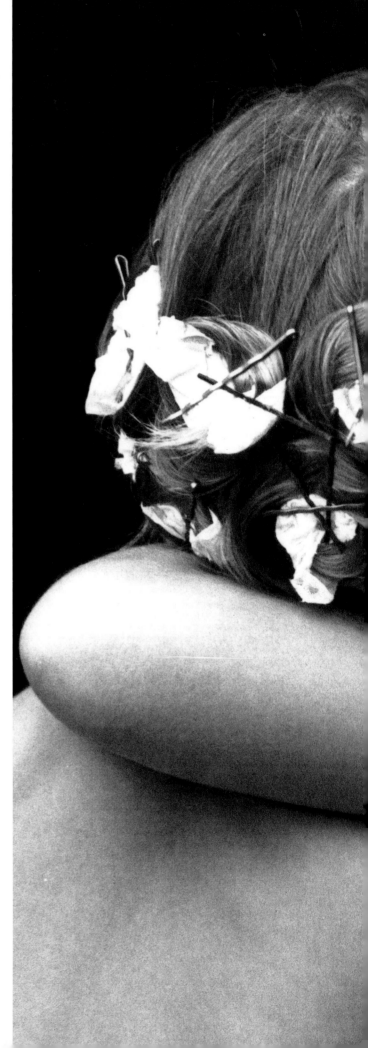

In this age of images in which we live, "picture books" have become commonplace. But this one is set apart. The photos in it were taken, essentially, not by practiced professionals but by the readers of *Parade* magazine, who, by their very number—more than 65 million—constitute a cross-section of the American people. And the subject the book celebrates, "The American Woman," has rarely been presented pictorially with such range, variety and imaginativeness. If there is such a thing as a "true image," then I believe it is here: how the American people—that is, our readers— see The American Woman today.

This photo competition, like our previous "We the People" Bicentennial contest, is a reflection of our interest in the lives and achievements of everyday people. As a Sunday magazine read in more than one of every three homes in the United States, *Parade* carries articles by world-famous authors and journalists each week, touching all phases of human thought and activity, as well as pictures by the top photographers of our day.

But there is a time, we believe, for our readers to share more directly—and no better way than through a photo contest open to all, no matter what their experience or expertise. The American Woman competition, jointly sponsored by *Parade* and Kodak, offered no particular guidelines, suggestions or restrictions. The theme, we believed, would be self-explanatory. And so it proved.

For we, as well as our distinguished judges—photojournalist Eddie Adams, psychologist Dr. Joyce Brothers, author Alex Haley, actress Marlo Thomas and columnist Liz Smith—were amazed at the variety and scope of the pictures submitted. We received more than 115,000 entries from every state in the nation, and from these the judges selected (with great difficulty, they report) one hundred winning photographs.

Perhaps, upon reflection, we should have been less surprised by the enormous diversity and range represented by the photos submitted in the competition, for both the art of photography and the status of women have undergone tremendous changes in recent years. Photography has become readily accessible to all. Just as earlier generations proudly wielded the old box camera, so do contemporary men and women—not to mention children—confidently handle equipment capable of great sophistication and subtlety. And it's more than a matter of the huge technological advances in photographic equipment; along with it has come a great upsurge in originality, opportunity and enterprise. Just as today's cameras are "smarter" than ever, so are today's camera-users more artistic and creative.

Years ago, such a focus as The American Woman might have conjured up little more than images of domesticity or perhaps clothing fashions. How different it is today. As the pictures in this collection so vividly attest, there are almost no limits to what women can achieve, accomplish and master. Today, women are athletes, surgeons, police officers, firefighters, pilots, mechanics, business leaders, executives of every stripe. Yet no one looking at the pictures which follow can doubt that many women also retain a central role as the centerpiece of the American family.

Above all, what comes through in these pictures is a compelling sense of compassion and *involvement*. These are women who not only achieve much for themselves but who also care deeply about others. Observe how many of the pictures show women as they relate to their families, their friends, their workplace, their community. American women have found a way to affirm their own individuality—a phenomenon displayed nowhere more movingly or convincingly than in the beautiful collection of photographs that follows.

Walter Anderson

« If I were asked… to what the singular prosperity and growing strength of the American people ought mainly to be attributed, I should reply: To the superiority of their women. »

—Alexis de Tocqueville

« Let the world know you as your are, not as you think you should be, because sooner or later, if you are posing, you will forget the pose, and then where are you? »

—Fanny Brice

« I'll walk where my own nature would be leading—it vexes me to choose another guide… »

—Emily Brontë

« Where I was born and where and how I have lived is unimportant. It is what I have done with where I have been that should be of interest. »

—Georgia O'Keeffe

« Life was meant to be lived, and curiosity must be kept alive. One must never, for whatever reason, turn his back on life. »

—Eleanor Roosevelt

▶

"She just loves red, white and blue," say her neighbors of Hattie Weems, 77, photographed by Cindy Sandlin in Florence, Ala.

▶ ▶
On following page: "Her name is Crystal, and I saw her in front of an empty building in North Bergen, N.J.," says the photographer, Jose Hernandez.

◀
Mother, model, bodybuilder. Erika Andersch, 29, has won several bodybuilding competitions. Photo by Eric Scott Bloom of Shrewsbury, Mass.

▲

Haircut time: Cindy Schlager gives a trim to son Michael, 3, in Cameron Park, Calif. Photo by Jo Ann Knehans.

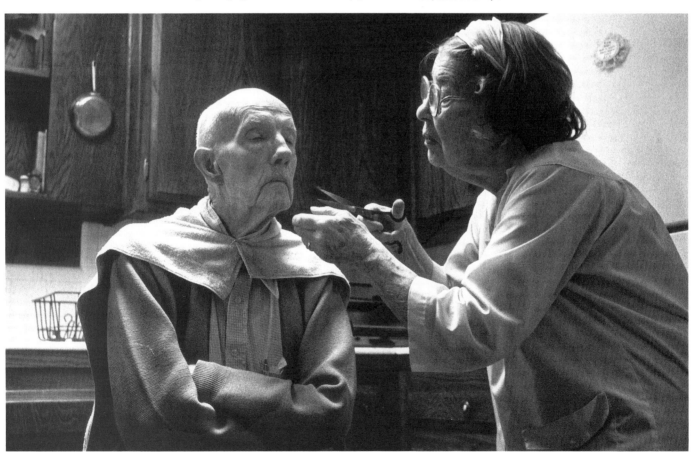

▲

Grandma still trims Grandpa's mustache—even after 56 years of marriage: Gail Soper, 90,
and wife, Elizabeth, 79, in the kitchen. Photo by their grandson, Caden M. Gray of Davis, Calif.

On previous page. Someone to be there: Foster grandmother Sybil Elkins, 80, gets a kiss from Jeffrey Lacoy, 3, at Merrimack Valley Day Care Service in Concord, N.H. Photo by Mandana Marsh Szkotak.

"Okay, Mom, if you say so." Amanda Lee McCurley, 1½, on Cape Cod with her mother, Cheryl, 23, of Marlboro, Mass. Photo by Laura Falcone Haupt.

▲

"Hey, Mom!" Five-month-old Brendan McNamara has a grin for his mother, Karen, in a toss-up during family vacation in St. Martin. Photo by Brendan's father, Sean, of Maplewood, N.J.

► Cradling her 3-year-old daughter, Taryn, Linda Seymour takes in the sun's last rays on the beach at Dennisport on Cape Cod. Photo by George B. Seymour.

▲

"Burning Down the House," or "Who's Minding the Flames?" These firepersons—Charmaine Holland, 21, and Mary Ellen Holland, 40 (front row, l-r), Hope Martin, 17, and Sharon B. Carr, 22 (back row, l-r)—are all members of the West Annapolis Fire Department. Photo by Joseph E. Handoe of Annapolis, Md., volunteer fire lieutenant and training officer. (The fire was just for practice.)

A lift for Edith Lucas: She's getting a ride on retired fire truck being used to deliver Christmas baskets. Edith was going to visit her sister-in-law, Pearlie Hyde, in a nursing home. Photo by Philip M. Grabill Jr. of Woodstock, Va.

▶
Fearless flyer: Skydiving
student Gloria Hanson,
44, makes her first
tandem free-fall jump
at 10,500 feet.
Instructor is Cliff
Dobson; photo is by his
son, Clifford P. Dobson.

Jane M. Simoni, a student at UCLA, set up this photo of herself skydiving for the first time in June 1988.

▲
Enforcer: Sandra Girvan—at 26, a policewoman for four years—at Strickland Range in Daytona Beach, Fla. Photo by Cheryl Farkas.

▶
Margaret Teresa "Aunty T" Donaldson, 83, of Hardy, Ark. "Though well-loved by the local folks, she knew how to use that squirrel gun," says the photographer, Barry Ellsworth French.

Do it this way: Emma Stracak, 95, shows the proper diving technique to her daughter, Elizabeth Takacs, 73, at the family pool in Tallmadge, Ohio. Photo by Katherine M. Cole of Tallmadge.

Mermaid: Gael Allegra, 31, of Salt Lake City swims
off Oahu, Hawaii. Photo by her husband, Michael.

▲
There are harder things in life: Anne Ponder Dickson takes a time-out during a houseboat vacation on Lake Powell, Ariz. Photo by her friend and fellow vacationer, Jody Polk Schwartz of El Paso, Tex.

Summer play: Jane E. Kimling took this photo of her mother, Mercedes, 58, swinging out over Lake Michigan from a launch platform near their campsite.

▲

Race day: Mindee O'Cummings, 15, finished first in her division in the 1988 "Kaiser Roll" in Bloomington, Minn. Photo by her mother, Patrice Cummings.

◄

Sisters in summertime: Britta Nicholson, 7, and sister Julia, 3, on the path to Pleasant Lake in North Oaks, Minn., where they live. Britta was born with spina bifida, the most commonly occurring birth defect, according to her mother, Barbara. Mrs. Nicholson adds that, aside from Britta's inability to walk, "she leads a perfectly normal life." Photo by the girls' father, David.

▲
We did it! Kathy Cytron (left) and Judith Weiss can still smile after finishing the
3400-mile TransAmerica Bicycle Trek. Photo by Shmuel Thaler of Santa Cruz, Calif.

▲

Diane Rose, 31, delivers a slow pitch during a women's
league game in Raritan, N.J. Photo by Howard Smock.

44

◄

Mirror image:
Gymnastics coach
Jeannie McCarthy
demonstrates the
balance-beam split—
upside down—to her
student, Laura Carlson,
8, of Aurora, Colo.
Photo by Laura's
mother, Deborah.

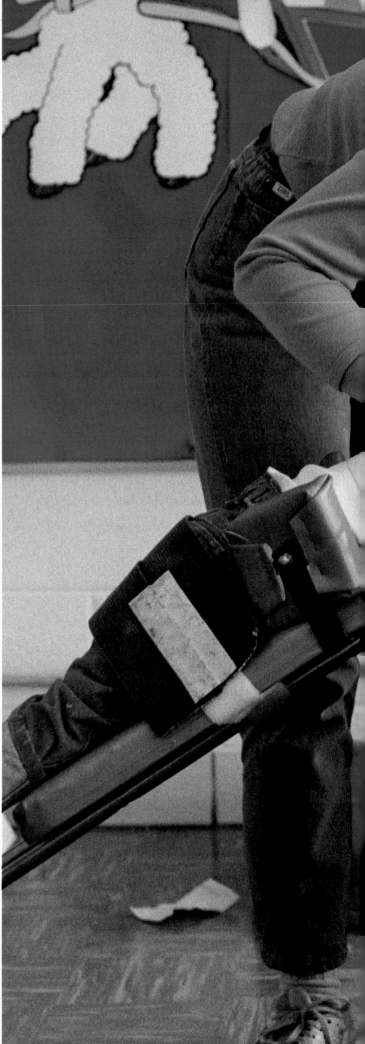

Jean Belding works with two impaired 3-year-olds at Cloverdale Training Center in Michigan. Photo by Ann Marie Belobradich-Smith.

▲

Music lesson: Ellen Carter instructs her class at the Longwood Elementary School in Hayward, Calif., with the help of Erin Devlin and a hand puppet. Photo by Susan Self.

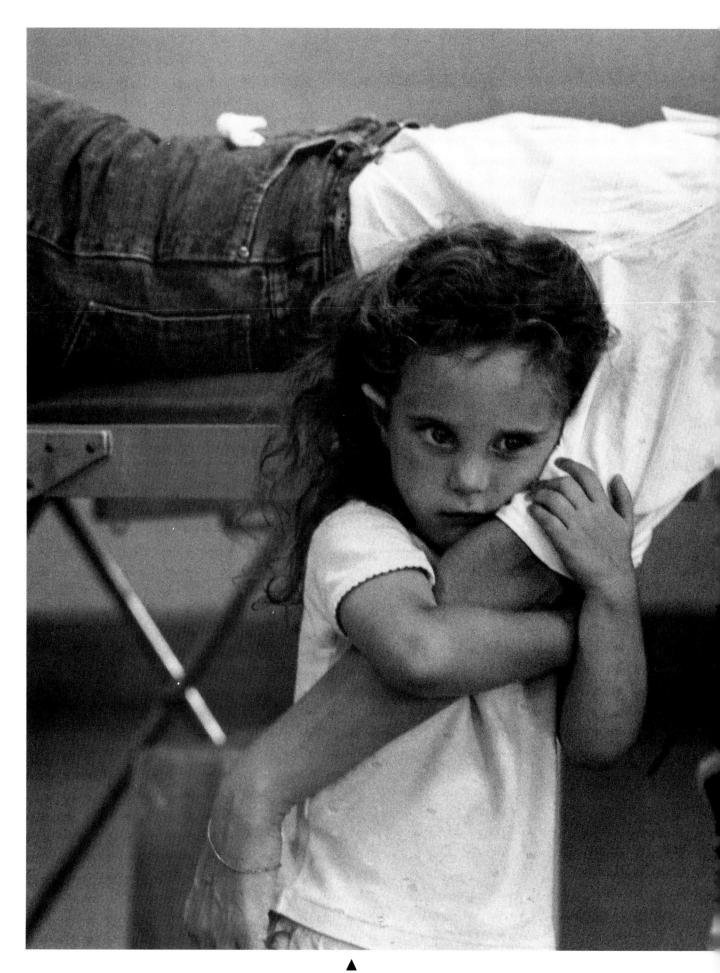

On a summer evening, Jessica Blanchard, 3, comforts her mother, Vicki,
who has just given blood at a donor drive in Dudley, Mass. Photo by Tim Collins.

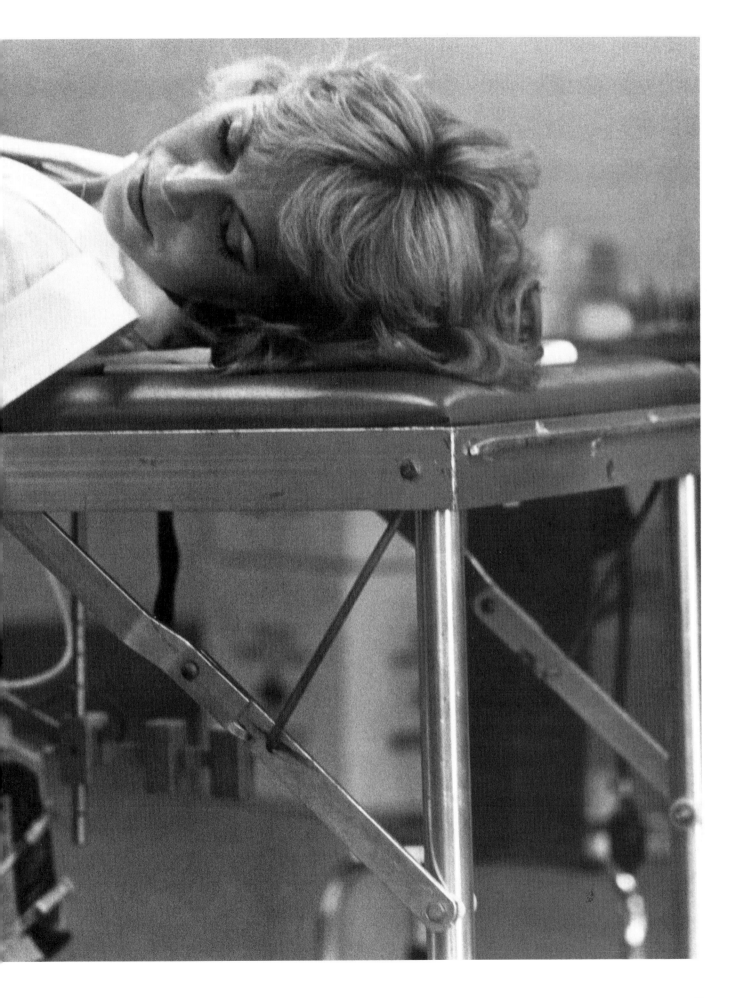

► City meets country: Patti Jones Quinn, 35, president of her own advertising and public-relations firm, joins her mother, Bettie Lacek Jones, 62, in the chicken house in Commerce, Ga. Photo by Patti Jones Quinn of Hull, Ga.

Amy Margaret Dykens, an artist and fisherwoman, in offshore action in Chatham, Mass. Photo by Nordel A. Gagnon.

Shelia Wilson, 13, works out in a group-skills project in Hampton, Va. Photo by Daniel R. Kooi.

▲
What are friends for? Sydney Joy Brumidis,
35, lends a hand to the photographer, Karen
Roberts of San Diego, who just moved into her new
home.

56

►
Jennifer Palmer, 20, and fellow Coast Guard cadet
David Semnoski, 19, store mooring lines. Photo by
Edward John Haukkala of New London, Conn.

Best friends: Deanna Jacoby (left) and Ramona
Kistler, friends since first grade, have a snack at
a summer event planned by Northern Lehigh
High School to introduce field-hockey players to
parents. Photo by Debra E. Smith of Neffs, Pa.

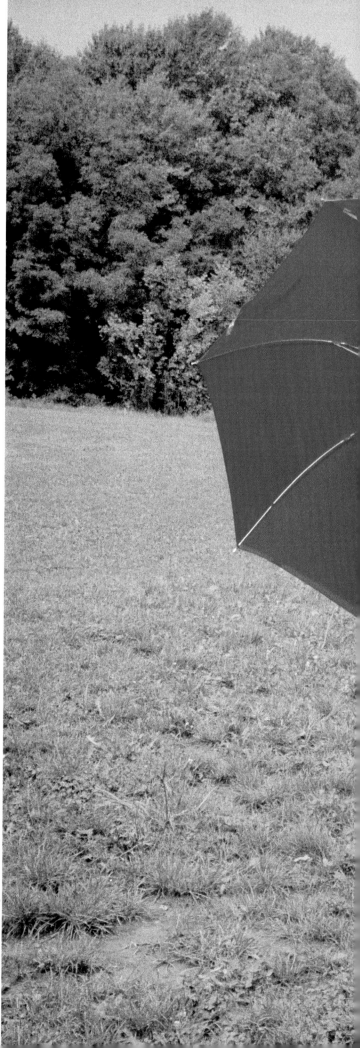

Julia (left) and Cecile, who both live in Coleman,
Wis., were in Twinsburg, Ohio, to attend an
international convention of identical twins. Photo
by Pauline Laybourn of Burnsville, Minn.

▲

Do they like each other? Maybe: Grandmother Mary Galloway, 60, regards grandson, Michael Morgan Galloway, 2, in the backyard while he has a snack. Photo by Mary's daughter and Michael's aunt, Julie Galloway Yanchulis of Alexandria, Va.

▲
One lump or two?—Ladies at teatime: Rachel
Collector, 3, prepares to pour for sister
Samantha, 22 months. Photo by their mother,
Susan, of Hermosa Beach, Calif.

▶
Play ball or play house? Future American woman
Kelly Wills, 2, shares her thoughts with
brother Tommy, 4. Photo by their mother, Janese
J. Wills of Smithsburg, Md.

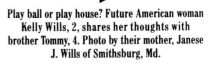

Sadie Wilcox and Erica Gilbert go out for a fly ball on an autumn afternoon in Amherst, Mass. Photo by Bruce G. Wilcox, Sadie's father, who says, "Not only are the girls good friends, but both were born on Oct. 27, 1977—by their calculations, 14 minutes apart."

▼

Grandchildren too numerous to count: Vernie Gilliam, at age 77, on the porch of her home in John's Creek, Ky. She's a mother of eight who still draws water from a well. Photo by Rick Tropp of Liberty, N.Y.

◄

Just a little cabin in the woods: Alison Hanshaft, 23, surrounded by the greenery of Maryland near Chesapeake Bay. Photo by Edwin P. Huddle of Lancaster, Pa.

" *God is a Mother.* **"**

—Eugene O'Neill

" *...mothers of the race, the most important actors in the grand drama of human progress...* **"**

—Elizabeth Cady Stanton

" *When a child enters the world through you, it alters everything on a psychic, psychological and purely practical level...And it's not the same again. Ever.* **"**

—Jane Fonda

" *My mother wanted me to be her wings, to fly as she never quite had the courage to do. I love her for that. I love the fact that she wanted to give birth to her own wings.* **"**

—Erica Jong

" *A mother is not a person to lean on, but a person to make leaning unnecessary.* **"**

—Dorothy Canfield Fisher

◄

Home from work: Shelly Kelly, a police officer in Olean, N.Y., greets daughter Colleen, 9 months. Photo by Geraldine Flicker.

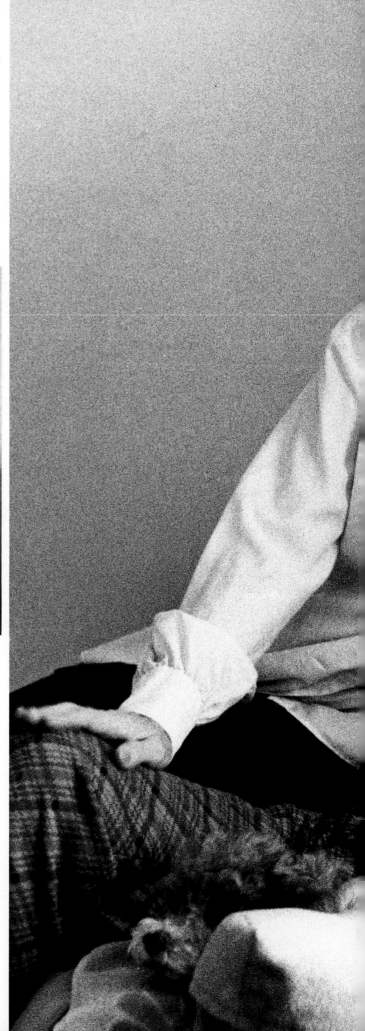

A daughter with her father: Jean Ann Berrier and Ward Townsley at his home in Dallas. Photo by Stephen Charles Cabrero.

A moment alone: In town for a visit, Adelia Parker gazes out window of Chicago's Allerton Hotel. Photo by Katie Knight of Ahmeek, Mich.

▲
Salt of the earth: Katherine Hutchinson, 82, on same farm in the
Piedmont region of South Carolina where her father and grandfather lived. Photo by Jonas N. Jordan of Pooler, Ga.

▲

Bini Abbott on her ranch in Arvada, Colo., with two of her miniature donkeys.
Photo by Susan R. Goldstein.

A hardworking woman: Alberta Cornelious—in her seventh year at Nottingham Brothers farm in Nassawadox, Va.—takes time out. Photo by Robin Layton.

▲
Pioneer: At her Idaho ranch, Daisy Erma Tappan
(1908-84) split wood, raised sheep and goats and
smoked cigarillos. Photo by Molly O'Leary Cecil.

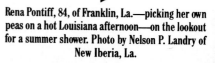
▶
Rena Pontiff, 84, of Franklin, La.—picking her own
peas on a hot Louisiana afternoon—on the lookout
for a summer shower. Photo by Nelson P. Landry of
New Iberia, La.

Reyesita, an American Indian in her 80s, at Taos Pueblo in
New Mexico. Photo by Jill Fineberg of Santa Fe, N.M.

Cecilia Robinson, an 85-year-old Chippewa Indian,
posed for a portrait at the Fond du Lac Reservation
in Minnesota. Photo by Prof. Joseph Boudreau.

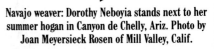

Navajo weaver: Dorothy Neboyia stands next to her
summer hogan in Canyon de Chelly, Ariz. Photo by
Joan Meyersieck Rosen of Mill Valley, Calif.

▲
Mary Bell "MarMar" Darwin of Fort Worth, Tex.
Photo by her granddaughter, Cheryl Susan Copeland.

"To be, or not to be": Eva Loseth, a drama student at Bradley University, by James G. Brey of Peoria, Ill., a photographer for the university.

▲
Fresh and natural: Tania Rountree, 24, strikes a
pose for the photographer, Steve Weiner, in his
studio in Manhattan.

Lyndsey A. Harris from Richmond, Va., is backlit
by the midmorning sun in Cancun, Mexico. The
picture was taken by her husband, Robin M.
Harris.

▲

Graduation day: Bridget Cresto, 31, and son Joseph, 2½, celebrate Mom's new master's degree. Photo by John J. Cresto.

◄

Elizabeth Walters, 21, celebrates her graduation from Colgate University in Hamilton, N.Y., in May 1987. Photo taken by her mother, Linda Walters of Haverford, Pa.

▲

Leslie Duff, 27, and daughter Sheena, 3, of Ramona, Calif., three days before the birth of Sheena's new brother, Laurence Lloyd Duff IV. Photo by Candy S. Fiddes.

◄

Stretching for two: Marla Rochlin, 29, of Santa Monica, Calif., takes exercise class a week before the birth of her daughter, Danielle. Photo by Timothy F. Moriarty III.

▲

Sisters get together: Mary Schreiner (left) with Meredith Schreiner Maclay and Sara Schreiner Kendall at parents' home in Great Falls, Va. All are in their 30s. Meredith and Sara each gave birth to boys. Photo by their brother, Peter, of West Hollywood, Calif.

▲

First Christmas: Julie Foran, 6 months, smiles up at her mother, Jan. Julie's outfit is a gift from her aunt, Debra L. Hinkle, the photographer, who traveled from Arlington, Va., to Dallas so the family could spend the holiday together.

Baby blue angel: 3-month-old Alexandra Wakeman of Austin, Tex.,
on Mokuleia Beach in Hawaii. Photo by her mother, Meg Wakeman.

Matriarch: Mrs. Noel B. "Momma Noel" Murray. 66, with her 26 grandchildren at
family reunion in Big Canoe, Ga., in June 1987. Photo by Pattie Murray.

Wedding gowns and chauffeur-driven cars may go together, but Darcy Seeger wanted a picture of herself on Dad's tractor in Boyceville, Wis. Photo by Judith Utphall.

▲
Sister Catherine Marie rides a tractor at Corpus Christi Monastery
in Menlo Park, Calif. Photo by Sister Mary of the Holy Spirit.

Fill 'er up: Marsha Hutchinson performs a little self-service
at a gas station in Lafayette, Ind. Photo by James Alkire.

A timeless moment in rural Le Sueur County, Minn.: Ila Grams, 77, mowing the grass on a summer afternoon, captured in a photo by Nancy J. McLain.

Image of two women: Doris Wadsworth, 64, who is blind, has her face turned to the window while her mother, Dora, 93, sits in the kitchen of their home in Appleton, Maine. Photo by Shelley Rotner of Northampton, Mass.

School bus driver Winnie Leischer prepares to pick up four steady customers on a farm in Loveland, Colo. Photo by Gale J. Sauer.

◀◀
On previous page. At
dusk, after some
thundershowers, the
light at California's Tule
Lake made colors glow
with richness. Araina
Gehr let her eyes roam
the landscape. Photo by
Bethany Dougher.

◀
The wind in the Blue
Ridge Mountains began
blowing as Ivy Zabicki
posed for a portrait.
She turned the event
to advantage, striking
a dancer's pose. Photo
by Stanley Zabicki.

◀

Now for a snuggle:
Lizanne Hennessey, 2,
gets all wrapped up
with Kate Purwin
Tschernisch during visit
to harbor's edge in
Quissett, Mass. Photo
by Lizanne's mother,
Sara Purwin Hennessey
of Seattle.

A funny face from Demi Peterson, who qualified for
the Miss Illinois Pageant by becoming Miss
Macomb. Photo by Lois P. Nicholson.

Grandmother Beatrice Sims, 67, gives an extra set
of ears to her grandson, Nathan Sims, 5 months, as
they pose in the Endless Mountains of Eagles Mere,
Pa. Photo by Beatrice W. Sims.

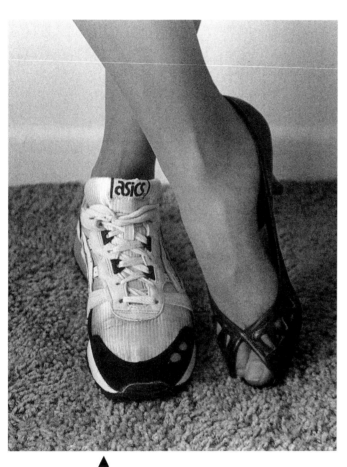

In step at work and at play: A self-portrait by
Evelyn R. Rib Gosnell of Miami, Fla.

Mary Grove, 22, holds an important phone
conversation. Photo by her sister, Barbara Grove of
San Francisco.

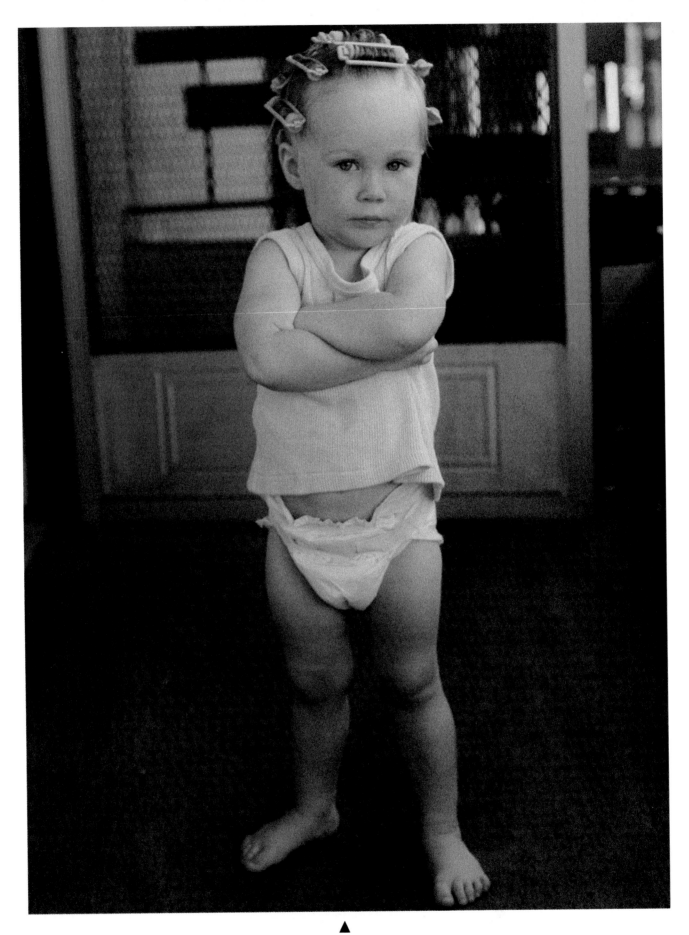

▲
"No, I won't!" Megan Mosley, 2, takes a stand in
front of her apartment building in Upland, Calif.
Photo was taken by her father, Kenneth, who
says, "Megan is a natural poser. She's bound to be an actress."

112

Lady Rebecca: Lorie A. Ellis of Tucson, Ariz.,
needed a model for a photography-class assignment
using window light, and her daughter Rebecca,
6, was happy to dress for the job.

▲
Privacy at last: With a storm about to break, one last sunbather has beach to herself near Panama City, Fla.
Photo by Kathy Wilkins.

►►
On following page: Into the sunset: Rebecca Winkler-Kostedt and her sons, Beau and Alex, stroll in sea off
Sanibel Island, Fla. Photo by William Kostedt.

▲
"This was The American Woman, and I felt
privileged experiencing the moment," said the
photographer on seeing Verna Jackson, 53, with her
grandchild, Mary Louise, 4, in Sandersville, Ga.
Photo by Kevin R. Schochat.

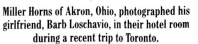
Miller Horns of Akron, Ohio, photographed his
girlfriend, Barb Loschavio, in their hotel room
during a recent trip to Toronto.

She knows a hymn or two: Myrtle ("Granny") White, 92, at the organ in her Phoenix home. Photo by Art Clark of Tempe, Ariz.

Listen to the music: Ann Houston plays the violin for daughter Marianna, 3, at Capitol Hill block party in Washington, D.C., in September 1987. Photo by Lois Kochanski of Bethesda, Md.

◄

Bride Marjorie Muirden walks with her attendants to an outdoor wedding ceremony at the Cathedral of the Pines in Rindge, N.H. Photo by John Gresock.

Just married: Anne Elkin, 25, looks up and has her picture
snapped by a wedding guest, Tracy Fox of La Mesa, Calif.

▶
Snow King stomp: Darci
and Kenny Lavitz whoop
it up shortly after
getting married atop
Snow King Mountain in
Jackson, Wyo. Photo by
Kenny's father, Irv
Lavitz of Winchester, Va.

▲
Wedding day: Bride-to-be Donna Wrolstad makes
final preparations in her mother's bedroom in
Portland, Ore. Photo by Mark S. Barnes.

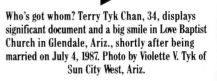

▶
Who's got whom? Terry Tyk Chan, 34, displays
significant document and a big smile in Love Baptist
Church in Glendale, Ariz., shortly after being
married on July 4, 1987. Photo by Violette V. Tyk of
Sun City West, Ariz.

◄ ◄

On previous page. Mary Roberts, co-owner of Sheep Mountain Cattle in Loomis, Wash., pursues a longhorn that has broken from the herd. Photo by Robin L. Barker of Issaquah, Wash.

On the Fourth of July in Mascalero, N.M., the day is celebrated with the Apache Indian Rodeo. One of the events is the barrel race. Photo by Stephanie Simmons.

"Who knows what women can be when they are finally free to become themselves? Who knows what women's intelligence will contribute when it can be nourished without denying love?"

—Betty N. Friedan

"I can do anything, because everything is allowed."

—Meryl Streep

*"If I have to, I can do anything.
I am strong, I am invincible,
I am woman."*

—Helen Reddy

*"I have met brave women who are exploring the outer
edge of human possibility, with no history to guide them, and
with a courage to make themselves vulnerable that
I find moving beyond words."*

—Gloria Steinem

"One can never consent to creep when one feels an impulse to soar."

—Helen Keller

◄

Patty Ballay enjoys the
quiet of an April sunset
at the Old Mill Pond in
McLean, Va. Photo by
Roger J. Ballay.

▲

Free spirit: E. Janine
Schooley, 30, of San
Diego, on Maui, Hawaii.
Photo by her husband,
Wilson Adam Schooley.

▲

All in good time: Sharrel Jean Souza, 41—expecting her first baby
—fishes at Sand Island off Oahu, Hawaii. Photo by her husband, Michael B. Souza.

◄
A dancer and a student at the University of Chicago.
Photo by Debra R. Sanders of Denver.

I think women are the most beautiful, the most powerful and the most complex creatures in the world. They are also the most difficult to photograph.

I think women are complicated, and their bodies and faces are complicated when you go to photograph them. There are a lot of lines, not just facial lines, and dealing with them, lighting your subject—probably the most important thing in photographing a woman, the light should be very very soft, and I like the colors to be pastel—these are some of the most difficult things in photography. Sometimes, for me, it's almost mystical. And when you get a good picture of a woman, that's almost mystical. You've really done it.

This is one of the main reasons why I was so impressed with the thousands of pictures that came into PARADE as part of the American Woman Photo Contest— that they contained so many really good pictures of women. Especially when you realize that most of them were taken by amateurs. Sometimes you can get lucky taking a photo, but I also know that all those entries weren't the result of sheer luck. Thousands of people really had some pretty good ideas of what they were doing.

This amazes me, especially when I consider how hard it is to get good pictures like that. I have thought and thought about it. One explanation that occurred to me was that you have to understand, to know your subject really well, I believe, to get an outstanding photograph: Your subject has to be unself-conscious, she has to be relaxed and ignoring the camera. That's why the women in these pictures don't care about posing, and aren't

even trying. They know their photographers as friends or relatives, and it's just another picture. At least that's how I see it.

I always get asked for pointers when I get involved in judging contests like this, and my best advice this time around has been: Just look at the pictures. Note how in the best of them the background is so clean—clear skies, a plain wall or a solid block of color. You don't want lamps growing out of heads, or furniture or a tree or a telephone pole sticking out of someone's body. You don't want anything to be cluttered.

Another thing I've noticed is that women tend not to know how to hold their hands in a photograph. All the fingers should always be separated, and there should be a little curl in the hand. That way they look very, very nice. Another thing is, your average person has a habit of standing too far back when he or she takes a picture. I like people's faces, so I move in awfully tight. I am fascinated by the face. Fill your viewfinder with your subject. Leave out the unimportant elements, but be sure you get the top of the head in. That's an important element.

It's easy to see that the people out there with cameras really are learning their stuff and also that they're smart enough to pick or place their subjects in settings that characterize them really well, that bring out the best in them, like in the shot of the older woman cutting the grass with a handmower or old "Aunty T" with her squirrel gun. They're completely relaxed and the camera catches them as you might see them any day, any time, any place. The camera catches them at an intimate moment. Intimate is an important word here.

Eddie Adams

140

H elen Reddy's theme song, "I Am Woman," played over and over in my mind as I sorted through dozens of the remarkable images submitted for PARADE's American Woman Photo Contest. Looking at them, I kept thinking: I am woman—I can do anything.

Psychologists all over the world would agree that, if you had a choice before birth today, you would choose to be born male—everywhere *except* in the United States. Being a male anywhere else is so much better, but here in our country the doors have been opened. For the first time in history, it is possible for a woman to be or do anything she wants.

In fact, it may be even harder now in this country to raise little boys than it is to raise little girls. A mother can let her little girl do anything, including things that, in the past, she would not have been allowed to do, from taking a clock apart or going out to play Little League baseball. But if you raise your little boy to be sensitive and caring and tender, all of which clearly are human traits and not the properties of one sex or another, you run the risk that, somewhere along the way, he's going to run the risk of being beaten up by a bunch of bigger males who haven't been raised to be sensitive and caring and tender.

When I look at these pictures, I can see how far we've come in celebrating the glory of being a woman. We still have a long way to go to reach economic parity, but that doesn't show in these photos. What does show is the joy, the tenacity, the giving, the diversity, the enthusiasm and the energy that women are experiencing today.

Women have always been asked to be the giving ones but now they are also the receiving ones. There are so many women today who are raising families as single parents and doing such an excellent job under difficult if not arduous circumstances, and this is one more dimension that some women have in their lives. In these pictures, women are equal partners with their men, but they don't need to form a partnership. There is an independence, a stalwartness, that comes across.

Dr. Margaret Mead said you can't have it all, but you can have some of it all at different times—and these pictures show women doing just that.

Dr. Joyce Brothers

These pictures together represent the most graphic and visual display I have seen of the thrust for the advancement of women. I don't mean so much the thrust for women's liberation, but for women maturing and expanding to become in so many more ways part of the world around us and the things that are being done in that world.

You see in this collection women who are healthy and beautiful— beautiful not in the ordinary sense of the word, but in so many other more comprehensive senses. They really give you a great sense of the roots of this country, ranging as they do from little girls to matriarchs.

There is a spirit of joy that comes from these pictures— mothers celebrating their children and vice versa, grandmothers reveling in their grandchildren, women of all ages and stages enriching their lives and those of others.

These, of course, are perennial themes that are all around us. But here they are concentrated in one set of pictures—a true look at women in America today.

Alex Haley

Some of these pictures are instructive, some are touching and some strike you to the heart. Some have a lot to say about women's liberation—they show women doing things we once would have regarded as offbeat, but not any more! They show women *doing* things, competing in sports, succeeding at jobs.

Many have much to say about old people and little children. People prize the juxtaposition of the generations, and these pictures show it. The sociology is impressive, like the theme of lonely black women sitting in depressing rooms, a dynamic statement about poverty.

Of course, there are fun pictures, too—fun because you've had similar experiences yourself. And it's delightful to have the celebrations of weddings and graduations—the records of the incomparable thrills of a lifetime, images of supreme joy.

I like all of my 100 pictures very much. It's trite but true for me to say that I'm sorry all the entries couldn't have been winners. I would love for the public to see what we have seen.

Liz Smith

L ooking at the faces of the women in these
photographs is like reading a richly detailed
biography of someone you know and,
simultaneously, like starting an intimate
conversation with a stranger.

Whether looking at family albums discovered in the attic or
the well-known photographs of Dorothea Lange, I have always
loved best the photographs that evoke a range of emotional,
rather than solely intellectual, responses. These photographs
do that. They show females of all ages absorbed in their lives—
from little girls giggling together to an old woman alone mowing
her lawn. Each one seems to tell a complete story: Of adventure,
courage, love, humor, solitude or shared experience.

Many of the photographs reveal women's compassion for
others. In those photos the camera has captured an essential
gesture, an attitude, a quality or caress that is a uniquely female
way of protecting or connecting with others.

The power of this collection is that the photographs are only
of women. Their faces radiate a warmth that is familiar. I see
my mother, my grandmother, my nieces and many women I
know in these faces. I also see myself. To look at these
photographs is to truly see the 'family of woman.'

Marlo Thomas